WOLVERHAMPTON on Wheels

Simon Dewey
and
Ned Williams

URALIA PRESS
1991

23 Westland Road, Wolverhampton, West Midlands, WV3 9NZ.

Wolverhampton On Wheels
ISBN 0 9511223 6 3

Uralia Press
23 Westland Road, Wolverhampton, WV3 9NZ.
Spring 1991.

Cover Design: Roger Crombleholme
Typesetting: James Quirke
Photo-processing: Jan Endean and Galata Print
Printed in Wolverhampton by Gibbons Barford Print.

ISBN 0 9511223 6 3

Cover photographs:
1. Len Crane's Fowler steam road locomotive (17212 of 1929) at Banks Brewery Centenary burying of a time capsule, 14 May 1990. (Ned Williams)
2. Wolverhampton Corporation No.580, a "tin-fronted" Guy Arab with MCW body stands parked in Railway Street, resplendent in its apple green and promrose livery, in 1963. (Simon Dewey)
3. Ex GWR "County" class 4-6-0 No.1024, "County of Pembroke", standing at the coaling stage at Stafford Road shed in the Spring of 1963. (Doug Nicholson)
4. Juliet Barnes waves from the platform of Wolverhampton trolley bus No.433, in Queen Square, in a painting by Haydn Smith.
5. Cover of a 1932 Wolf motor cycle catalogue, from the collection of Jim Boulton.

Introduction

Once upon a time wheels played a major part in the life of Wolverhampton. Even before the coming of the railway there was a local industry concerned with horse-drawn vehicle maunfacture. But when the railways did arrive, Wolverhampton became a "railway town", not just a place the railways passed "en route", but a town where locomotives were built, locomotives were shedded, goods trains were marshalled, carriages prepared for their next duties, and goods traffic transferred between road and rail, or between canal and rail. Our manufacturing industries turned to the production of tramway equipment, cycles, motor cycles, commercial and passenger-carrying vehicles and private cars. The town has played its part in building everything from milk floats to record cars, and when we have not built the "final product", we have made components for other people's products.

This book celebrates Wolverhampton's association with wheels in just over ninety photographs, chosen for their rich variety rather than in any attempt to be comprehensive. We know there are omissions, but the selection has been a personal one, and our aim is to whet your appetite! It's not just a matter of liking certain locomotives or vehicles, it is also a matter of liking certain photographs and pursuing particular themes, or even a wish to share certain collections of pictures that have not appeared in print before.

In 1978 and 1983 we produced "Wolverhampton Railway Albums, Volumes I and II". Both are "out-of-print", and technical problems make new editions unlikely, although there may be scope for a "Wolverhampton on Rails" to follow this book! The "Railways of the Black Country" volumes are also out-of-print. This is the situation that has led to the desire to be back in print with local transport pictures, and the quest for a new formula. Meanwhile, others have made a contribution to putting the Wolverhampton transport scene onto the printed page. John Bates and Mervyn Strodzinsky produced six editions of the "Wolverhampton Railway Gazette", which put before us many new interesting pictures of Wolverhampton's railways. In 1990 Paul Collins produced "Wolverhampton" in the Ian Allan "Rail Centre" series, an example of being "put on the map" by a national publisher!

In the world of road transport there have been books on individual manufacturers, and books in which local bus fleets have been featured. Jim Boulton has disseminated his knowledge of local manufacturers in "Powered Vehicles Made in the Black Country" (Black Country Society, 1990.) In 1986 the Birmingham Transport Historical Group published the first volume of "A History of Wolverhampton Transport" (1833 - 1930), in which Stan Webb and Paul Addenbrooke brought to completion the work started by Osmond Wildsmith.

Wolverhampton's transport, both road and rail, has had many enthusiastic followers, many of whom showed great devotion to the cause, and considerable talents in the written and photographic records they created. In some ways this enthusiasm and talent has been rejected or squandered by "officialdom", in the sense that the town's council has a bad record of exploiting the transport elements of the town's heritage. Great opportunities were missed in the 1960s in an age of innocence, but in the 1980s and 1990s we are supposed to have learnt the value of preserving the best of our past in order to promote the town's identity and its future. When Wolverhampton celebrated its Millennium in 1985, we looked forward to the day when the town's transport history would play its part in bringing visitors and investment to Wolverhampton. We are still waiting.

Photographs found in a book like this are assembled between these covers as the result of the generosity of many people. Sometimes the pictures are found in vast collections, sometimes it is a matter of stumbling upon individual photographs, sometimes it is a matter of picking people's brains, or following-up their suggestions. One interesting collection of photographs was assembled by Phil Lycett (1922 - 1973). Phil lived in All Saints Road, and was introduced to an interest in transport by his uncle, William Phillips. Phil carried on this tradition by passing on the enthusiasm to his nephew, Johan Van Leerzum, who has made the photographic collection available to us. Phil Lycett was known all over the railway system and had access to many sheds and works. In Wolverhampton itself he took railway photographs, some we included in "Wolverhampton Railway Album Vol.1", and took a remarkable number of pictures of road transport, some of which we have been able to include in this book. Nowadays the possession of a camera is taken for granted, and colour prints must be accumulating in nearly every home at an alarming rate, and yet one seldom sees the kind of photograph that was taken by previous generations, and that is now so valuable in compiling a book such as this.

That is why we wish to say a big Thank you to the following:

John Bates   Roger Jennings
Jim Boulton   Peter Hough
Philip Eisenhoffer   Johan van Leerzum
John Hughes   Doug Nicholson
Dorothy Hughes   Dick Rhodes
Bert Bradford   Brian Robbins
Alex Chatwin   John Spittle
Les Clough   Cynthia Stuart
Len Crane   John Vaughan
Joe Davies   Claude Wright
Steve Everall   Wolverhampton Public Libraries

Jan Endean processed many of the photographs, and made prints available from the Eardley-Lewis collection.
While presenting an exhibition as part of the Wolverhamton Millennium celebrations, a collection of transport photographs was made available, and some of those pictures are reproduced in this book. Arthur Bennett Clark took many photographs for the Corporation, and prints of these pictures now turn up in many different places. We hope we have acknowledged photographs correctly and fairly - a task that becomes more difficult as time goes by, and pictures simply surface as part of someone's collection, and the photographer is unknown. We are always interested in seeing photographs that might contribute to a sequel!

Simon Dewey
Ned Wiliams.
Spring 1991.

1. The Royal Train at Low Level.

Wolverhampton Low Level station in the late 1890s, with the LNWR Royal Train of 1890 heading north, probably conveying Queen Victoria from Windsor to Balmoral. the train has arrived behind GWR No.14, "Charles Saunders", one of William Dean's small class of 4-4-0 engines of 1894. It is about to be exchanged for the LNWR engine seen in the bay platform. The latter, one of Webb's "Greater Britain" class, is almost certainly No.2054, "Queen Empress". The Dean engines were all transferred to the Wolverhampton Division after 1909, where they handled local traffic within the Northern section of the Great Western Railway. At the time the photograph was taken, both the High Level station, in the background, and the Low Level station, had all-over roofs, and the picture shows the proximity of the two stations.

(Dick Rhodes Collection)

2. Horse Bus at Penn.

The atmosphere of Wolverhampton's suburb of Penn in the days of horse-drawn traffic is captured in this scene at the Rose & Crown in the first decade of this century. On the right is Sampson Tharme's horse bus with its three horse team, driver, and conductor. The horse bus operated on this route from 1882 until 1910/11. The Rose & Crown building has been replaced twice since the time when this photograph was taken, and the Penn Road has become a fast-moving dual carriageway.

(A John Steen series postcard from the Eardley-Lewis Collection.)

3 Trolleybus Accident at Newbridge.

On 22 May 1946 Wolverhampton trolleybus 295 was returning to town from Tettenhall when it went out of control at Newbridge and plunged over the embankment close to the GWR Wombourne line. As soon as it came to rest Driver Hubbard rescued the passengers and Conductor Cahill, but retrieving the vehicle was more of a problem. The following day two of Pat Collins' showman's engines arrived to tow it back onto the road. On the left is "Mabon", (Burrell 2709 of 1904), brought from the Collins' Bloxwich Yard by Driver Billy Mills.

At the back is "Goliath", (McLaren 1623 of 1917), brought back from Newport Fair by Driver Jim Morley.

(Peter Hough Collection.)

4. An Aveling-Porter at John Thompson's.

The ex John Thompson crane engine (Fowler 17212 of 1929), now preserved by Len Crane, illustrated on the front cover of this book was purchased new by the firm, about 1929. Before that, John Thompson had used this Aveling Porter compound steam road locomotive, No.5322 of 1903. It is thought to have been scrapped about 1929. Thompson's Fowler performed works duties until about 1958, and was then steamed once more one weekend in 1960 to pose with the company's 10,000th boiler.

It stood idle for a further decade until purchased for preservation by Len Crane.

(Wolverhampton Public Libraries via P.Eisenhoffer.)

5. Steam Wagon Cavalcade.

J.N.Miller, the Wolverhampton miller took delivery of these five Foden steam wagons in the Autumn of 1928. (UK 6139, 6076, 6083, 6034, and one unidentified.) Foden Ltd., of Sandbach, had just introduced this new model to the market, using a vertical boiler, underfloor engine, pneumatic, or solid rubber, tyres and increased carrying capacity. The long-established mill still dominates the skyline by the High Level station, although its position was originally determined by access to the canal.

(Wolverhampton Public Libraries, via P.Eisenhoffer.)

6. May Day Parade, West Park.

Many users of horse-drawn delivery vehicles organised May Day Parades of their fleets. These dark green Wolverhampton & District Cooperative Society Bakery delivery carts are lined up outside West Park one May Day about 1930. Note that the Butchery Department's delivery boy and his bicycle appear to have won a rosette. The Wolverhampton & District Cooperative Society was created in 1885 and survived until 1972, when it was absorbed by the Walsall Society.

(Wolverhampton Public Libraries.)

7. May Day in Blakenhall.

On 1st May 1946 the Parade of the Wolverhampton & District Cooperative Society Bakery Department's vehicles was held near the Society's bakery in Blakenhall. On the right, the Society's Secretary and General Manager, S.H."Jack" Lewis, congratulates the winning horse, "Peggy", and her driver, J.Hillman. In the centre of the three figures on the right is Ben Wignell, from the LCS Dairy at Bridgnorth, who acted as judge of this annual competition for several years.

By this time the carts had acquired pneumatic tyres and the livery had become green and cream.

(Cynthia Stuart Collection.)

8. "Let the Laundry Do It All!"

Driver Les Clough at the wheel of a Morris Commercial van owned by the Wolverhampton Steam Laundry - outside the Company's Sweetman Street entrance to the Laundry about 1930. The laundry was started in 1890, and has just celebrated its centenary. The vans were immaculately turned out in a red, white and black livery, the drivers being responsible for keeping the van clean, as well as routine maintenance. The drivers were also "salesmen" for the laundry's services and were taught how to talk to customers from different social classes, and how to win the custom of each. The vans took part in parades and the Hospital Carnivals, and formed an impressive fleet of over twenty vehicles.

(WSL Collection)

9. Wolverhampton Police Ambulance.

This 1916 Star ambulance, DA 2992, was purchased after War-service by funds collected by the Special Constabulary, and was presented to the Chief Constable, David Webster. It was used until 1931, when it was replaced with a Morris Commercial vehicle. It is photographed outside the Royal Hospital, along with, from left to right: Fire Brigade Inspector Edwards, Police Inspector Albert Jones, Fireman Billy Penn, and P.C.77.- Jim Jones, the tallest constable in the force. Between the Wars the emergency services were provided by the Borough Police. Twentyfour policemen were paid an extra 2/- a week to be firemen, and received one extra pair of trousers. The Fire Department had two Dennis engines, and the Police had this Star ambulance, a Ford one ton prison van, one Clyno car, three AJS motorcycle combinations, and twelve bikes - six Sunbeams and six Wearwells.

(Wolverhampton Public Libraries)

10. Springfield Brewery Fire Brigade

Butler's Springfield Brewery, in Wolverhampton, had its own fire brigade assembled here with the horse drawn appliance just before the First World War. From left to right: T.Price, J.Willis, H.Birch, H.Turner, Mr.Cooper, T.Ambrose, G.Shelley, T.Appleby and A.Rendison. The photograph was "rediscovered" in 1946 and reproduced in Butler's Magazine.

(John Spittle collection)

11. A Fireman's Funeral

The funeral of Wolverhampton Fireman David Southwick took place on 22 July 1925, and in this photograph, his coffin is seen arriving at the West Door of St.Peter's Church on board one of Wolverhampton's Dennis fire engines. In the background, on the left, the Police band can be seen. David Southwick had given 21 years service to the local force, and the funeral was a major public occasion.

(F.Jennings & Sons)

12. F. Jennings & Sons 1.

In 1848 George Jennings first undertook the complete arrangements for a customer's funeral. He had been a skilled wood-worker whose craftsmanship was often devoted to the manufacture of coffins. With his wife's support, and administrative skills, he was able to expand the business to take on the whole organisation of funerals. Together they ran the business until their son, Frederick, was able take control in 1875. He eventually moved the business from the cottage-sized premises in Union Street, into better premises in St. James Street, Horsley Fields. Here there were stables, a coach house, and up-to-date workshops. His sons joined the business, as implied by the name, and took over when he died in 1916. Today the firm is still run by the same family, in the fourth and fifth generation, and can still provide a horse-drawn hearse if required. In this turn-of-the-century picture, Frederick Jennings sits beside the driver of the hearse, outside the premises at 16 St. James St.

(F. Jennings & Sons)

13. F. Jennings & Sons 2.

Two Austin hearses belonging to F. Jennings & Sons make their way through Leicester Square, Whitmore Reans, in the early 1930s. The company's first motor hearse was a Ford, and today they use Daimlers, but these Austins with there carved woodwork, and angled windscreens were rather elegant. The company had always been ready to adopt new modes of transport, and, for many years, used a bill head illustrating a horse-drawn hearse with separate compartment for the mourners.

(F. Jennings & Sons)

14. Wolverhampton Trams 1.

At the end of the last century several tramways were operated in Wolverhamton by private companies, using horse drawn trams, and cars pulled by steam "tram engines". The Corporation debated whether to take over the tramways, whether to operate the services themselves, and which system should be used to electrify the tramways. The Wolverhampton Corporation Act of 1899 gave the Council powers to acquire tramways, convert them to 3ft.6in. gauge, electrify, and operate them. On 1 May 1900 the Tramways Department took over, horse trams were decorated to mark the occasion and staff appeared in new uniforms. The controversy surrounding choice of methods of electrification continued. In the end the surface contact system, the "Lorain system" was adopted - giving the town's tramways a very distinctive and individual place in tramway history. In this picture one can see the first mile of experimental Lorain fitted track, completed in January 1902, in Cleveland Road, and opened on 6 February after intensive trials. In the distance the new tram depot has been built, and on the right are the premises of Forder's Carriage works, a reminder of Wolverhampton vehicle-building industry in horse-drawn times.

(Bert Bradford's collection)

15. Wolverhampton Trams 2.

When the Corporation ran its first electric trams early in 1902, they used three Lorain-supplied cars of different design, two single deckers and one double decker. The bodies were built by G.F.Milnes & Co. of Hadley, and were numbered 10, 11, & 12. In this picture single deck car No.12, and double deck car No.11 pose outside the new Cleveland Road Depot. They were fitted, experimentally, with Providence Lifeguards, which are displayed in the raised and lowered positions. The service down Cleveland Road to the junction with the Ettingshall Road began on 6 February 1902. The absence of overhead wires gives tram pictures of the Corporation's system a distinctive appearance.

(Bert Bradford's collection)

16. Wolverhampton Trams 3.

Driver Andrew Vaughan stands at the controls of Wolverhampton Corporation tramcar No.3, an open-top double decker built in 1902 by the Electric Railway & Tramway Carriage Works Ltd., on Brill trucks. The car is standing at the Bushbury Lane terminus of the line extended from Waterloo Road on 13 August 1904. The destination blind simply says "Raily.Station", as route numbers were not introduced until 1915.

(John Vaughan's collection)

17. Wolverhampton Trams 4.

Lea Road in the early 1920s. Wolverhampton Corporation double deck tramcar No.61 returns to town from the Penn Fields terminus. No.61, supplied in 1921, was one of the final batch supplied by English Electric to the Corporation. Note the trolley poles and span wires - the Penn Fields route was converted from the Lorain system to overhead current collection on 15 October 1921. The car is displaying the wrong route number, "1" instead of "4", suggesting that the new overhead system is undergoing trials. The trams ceased running to Penn Fields on 20 March 1927.

(Eardley-Lewis Collection)

18. Tramway Heyday

Wolverhampton tramcars in their depot in Cleveland Road in 1902, shortly after commencement of electric tramcar operation. No.19, supplied by the Electric Railway & Tramway Carriage Works Ltd., in August 1902, carries a destination blind for the "Exhibition" - Wolverhampton's famous 1902 Exhibition in West Park opened on 1 May, and the brand new electric tramway serving West Park and Whitmore Reans opened on the same day. Note that car no.17, built by Milnes, has a slightly different staircase. Once again the absence of overhead wires is very apparent. A 12ft. long skate collected the current from contact boxes placed in the roadway between the rails. These were only energised when the car passed over them. Tales of horses being electrocuted by treading on these contacts, or "studs" have never been authenticated.

(Millennium Collection)

19. Wednesfield Road Goods Depot.

Goods traffic borne by the railways has often had to be carried by local transport between the railway and the customer's door. Before the supremacy of the motor lorry this meant collections and deliveries by horse and cart, sometimes provided by the railway company, and sometimes by a local agent. The Midland Railway provided its own delivery service, as seen in this 1908 view of Wednesfield Road Goods Yard. The Goods and Grain Warehouse was completed in 1881 and still stands today.

(Wolverhampton Public Libraries.)

20. LMS Horse Drawn Parcels Van.

Horse drawn vehicles were seen on the streets of Wolverhampton well into the Post-War era. The railways were nationalised on 1 January 1948 but this LMS parcels van, 4990, is still carrying its LMS maroon livery on 18 September 1952. The vehicle is outside Craddock's Shoe Warehouse. This business was established by Stephen Craddock (1853 - 1925) who played a prominent part in the town's Tramways Committee.

(Tim Shuttleworth)

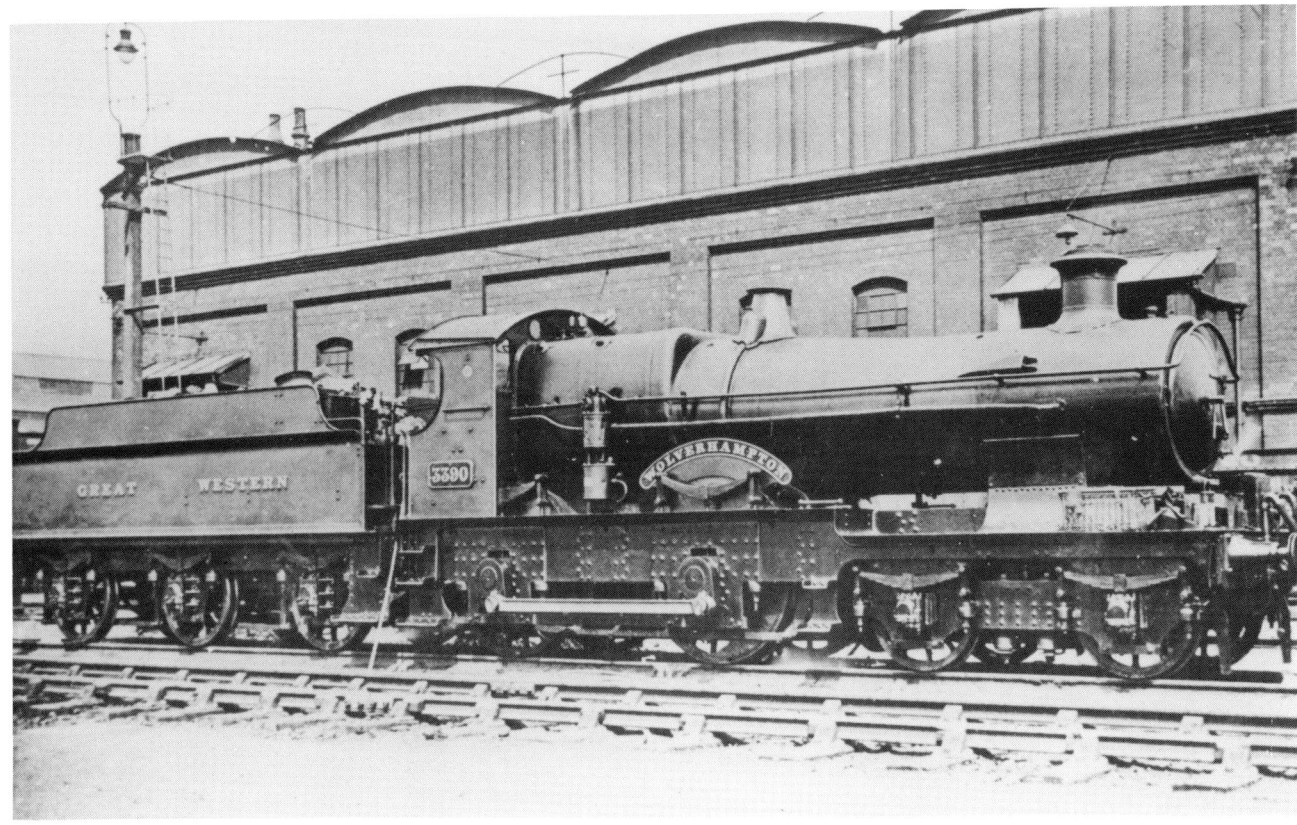

21. "Wolverhampton" on Wheels.

Originally numbered 3450, but renumbered 3390 in 1910, this GWR "Bulldog" class 4-4-0 locomotive, built at Swindon in 1903, was named "Wolverhampton", one of several similar locomotives named after places served by the GWR system. It has been alleged that passengers became confused between the name of the locomotive and the destination of the train, and all such engines lost their names in 1927. It must be said that other engines carried names such as "Australia" and "Calcutta", and one is left to wonder if these passengers believed that the GWR's area of operation extended to such places! "Wolverhampton" is seen here at Old Oak Common Shed, in London, about the early 1920s, unusually fitted with a Westinghouse air brake pump. The engine was withdrawn in 1939, but at least one nameplate has survived - now in the ownership of Wolverhampton Borough Council.

(Millennium Collection)

22. The Low Level Station.

The southern end of Low Level station in April 1962, seen from Sun Street bridge, with "King" class 4-6-0 No.6017 "King Edward IV" awaiting departure on an express to Paddington from the main Up platform. In the bay alongside the "King" is a push-pull auto-trailer powered by an 0-6-0PT, 6428, steam from the safety valve of which is seen rising above the station canopy. It will form a local working to Dudley. The Wolverhampton South Signal Box occupies the right foreground. Above this, in the background, can be seen the station's carriage sheds, with 84xx and 51xx class tank engines on duty. The station closed to passengers in 1972, but remained in use as a parcels depot until 1981. Although now a listed building, and an important part of the town's "Heritage Area", the station's future is currently uncertain. It belongs to the Black Country Development Corporation.

(Simon Dewey)

23. The High Level Station.

Unrecognisable when compared with its present form, the southern end of High Level station is seen here as it was in about 1961, before being rebuilt as part of the electrification of the LMS lines through the town. The all-over roof and semaphore signals were to be swept away. "Royal Scot" class 4-6-0 No.46126 "Royal Army Service Corps" leaves with an express towards Birmingham, and two types of diesel multiple unit are visible, of the type introduced on local train services at the end of the 1950s. In the background are lines occupied by a goods van and guard's van, these lines now form a locomotive stabling point - the nearest equivalent Wolverhampton now has to an engine shed!

(John Bucknall)

24. Turning an Engine in Oxley Shed.

The GWR's Oxley shed was opened in 1907, a substantial red brick building some 450ft. long, located adjacent to the Down side of Oxley Sidings, and provided to house freight and shunting engines, transferred from the overcrowded and older sheds at Stafford Road. The main building contained two turntables from which radiated lines on which locomotives were stored. The turntables were hand operated, were 65ft. in diameter, and could accommodate even the largest tender locomotives. A work-stained LMS class 5 4-6-0 No.45391, is seen being turned in February 1967, only weeks before the shed's closure. The last GWR locomotives had left the shed to be scrapped, and the shed's final allocation consisted of ex-LMS or BR type locomotives.

(Simon Dewey)

25. A Signalman's View of Oxley Sidings.

This was the view looking northwards from Oxley South Signal Box, in the mid 1920s. Oxley Engine Shed is just visible in the left background, and the main running lines of the GWR route to Shrewsbury are the clear parallel lines running through the centre of the picture. Sidings to the left of the running lines (on the Down side) were designated the "Crewe" and "Birkenhead" yards. Those on the right (the Up side) constituted the "Old Yard", "Middle Sidings" and the "New Yard". Two Up freight trains, one double-headed by a "Castle" class 4-6-0 and a 43xx Mogul, and the other by a Mogul only, await clearance to depart southwards. An open-cabbed 0-6-0PT stands by the water tower. In the centre of the picture is Dean Goods, 0-6-0 No.2385, and, in the distance, the signal indicates the road is clear for a northbound train.

(Millennium collection)

26. "Silver Jubilee" at Bushbury.

Pictures of the LMS in Wolverhampton are much rarer than pictures of the GWR, despite the fact that it is the LMS route to Wolverhampton that has survived. On 30 September 1935 the LMS introduced an express that left Euston at 9.15.am. and arrived at Birmingham New Street 1hr.55mins. later. The service was inaugurated by Driver Joe Cox of Bushbury Shed, driving LMS Class 5, 4-6-0 No.5552 "Sliver Jubilee". The locomotive, seen here at Bushbury, had been re-numbered in April 1935 and was painted in gloss black with chromed steel boiler bands, numbering and lettering. "Silver Jubilee" was then sent to various sheds as a "showpiece". Left to right: Fireman J.Cripps, Timekeeper Sid Newill, Driver Pat Malkin, and cleaners Len Turner and Wilf Shelton.

(Joyce Batchelor's collection via John Bates.)

27. One of Bushbury's Own.

Stanier "Crab" 2-6-0 No.42966, seen here in the shed yard in March 1963, was among Bushbury shed's latter day allocation of locomotives, and wears its 21C shedcode on its smokebox door accordingly. The shed was coded 3B up until 1960, 21C from then until 1963, and finally 2K until its closure in 1965. Unlike the GWR sheds at Stafford Road and Oxley, Bushbury possessed mechanical coaling and ash disposal facilities. The ash disposal tower, seen here in the background, along with the coaling plant, rivalled the factory chimney at Goodyear's for dominance of the local skyline. *(Simon Dewey)*

28. Built in Wolverhampton
Wolverhampton-built GWR 0-6-0ST, No.1040, seen here in the Lower Yard at Stafford Road. the engine was built in 1870, and was one of sixty locomotives of the "1016" class. Locomotives were built at the GWR's works at Stafford Road, from 1859 to 1908. Unfortunately, no examples of Wolverhampton-built locomotives have survived into preservation.

(Eric Hamilton collection)

29. Stafford Road Locomotive Works.
Wolverhampton was the headquarters of the GWR's Northern Division, and its locomotive workshops were second in importance only to Swindon. When locomotive building ceased in 1908, the work of locomotive repair continued, and the works was eventually much enlarged between 1929 and 1932. Repair work continued until the closure of the Works in 1964. Here, in 1960, a 2-6-2T locomotive is being lowered by an overhead crane onto its wheels during re-assembly after a major overhaul in the 1932 erecting shop.

(Eric Hamilton collection)

30. Stafford Road Coaling Stage.

The coaling stage at Stafford Road was sited well away from the shed yard, across the canal towards Cannock Road Junction. Here locomotives were turned on the turntable, coaled and watered, before retiring to the shed to await their next turn of duty. "Castle" class 4-6-0 No.5063, "Earl Baldwin" is seen standing on the approach to the coaler from the turntable, in the summer of 1963. 5063 was based at Stafford Road until the shed closed in September 1963, and was then re-allocated to Oxley until its withdrawal in February 1965. The coaler was a popular spot for railway photographers over a period of many years.

(Simon Dewey)

31. A "King" at Cannock Road Junction.

GWR "King" class 4-6-0 No.6021, "King Richard II" is seen easing forward from the up to the down lines at the crossover just south of Cannock Road Junction signal box in the summer of 1962. The engine had brought an express from Paddington to Wolverhampton, the coaches of which it had just deposited in Cannock Road Coach Sidings, and is just completing its manoeuverings in order to gain access to Stafford Road shed for servicing. At the end of the Summer timetable in 1962 the "Kings" ceased their reign over the Paddington expresses, and 6021 was withdrawn and consigned to the scrapheap. *(Simon Dewey)*

32. Not a Bare Head in Sight.

We believe this to be a Mutual Improvement class of local GWR employees, posing for their formal photograph in front of GWR "Star" class 4-6-0 No.4067, "Tintern abbey", in the shed yard at Stafford Road, probably during 1923, the year the locomotive was built. The viaduct dominating the background carries the LMS Stour Valley line northward towards Bushbury. Mutual Improvement classes were held for the benefit of company servants in the GWR Railwaymen's Institute, at the southern end of Stafford Road Locomotive works. It was reached up a long flight of steps from the Stafford Road itself, and these steps survived until the recent widening of Stafford Road.

(Eric Hamilton Collection)

33. A Railwayman's Retirement.

Driver Arthur James Smith, on the day of his retirement, poses with the Stafford Road Shed Foreman Humpage, by his last charge, a GWR "King" class 4-6-0 No.6006, "King George I", on 6 June 1937. No.6006 was a Stafford Road locomotive for virtually all its life, and had the dubious distinction of being the first of the "Kings" to be withdrawn, in February 1962. At the time of this photograph it was a mere nine years old, and amongst the elite of the shed's allocation, its pristine condition testimony to its status and that of its driver, known, appropriately for a Wolverhampton man, as "AJS".

(Mike Thatcher)

34. Wheel Tapping at Bushbury Shed.

In an obviously posed photograph of the mid 1930s, the crew of LMS "Baby Scot" 4-6-0 No.5515, lean out of the cab as a wheel tapper checks the locomotive's central driving wheel, watched by the bowler-hatted shed foreman. Built in 1932, No.5515 was named "Caernarvon" in 1939, and the class of which it was a member became more popularly known as "Patriots" after the name of the first in the class. Bushbury Shed maintained a stud of passenger locomotives for use on the Wolverhampton - Euston trains, but the shed's fleet was always dominated by freight or mixed traffic locomotives. *(Eric Hamilton collection)*

35. Wolverhampton's "New" Railway Line.

After the cessation of through services via the Low Level station in 1967, the tracks north of the station were lifted from there to Cannock Road Junction. In a much rationalised form, Cannock Road Junction was then retained as a point at which trains could reverse when travelling between Bushbury Junction and Stafford Road Junction. The only trains needing to do so were the coal trains making their way to Buildwas Power Station from the Stafford line. In order to avoid this reversal a new "curve" was built, known as the "Oxley Chord". The new double-track line curves at a very tight radius from a point at which the GWR line used to cross the canal round to the old connecting line to Bushbury Junction, south of the Showell Road bridge. It came into use, without ceremony, in August 1983. Although built to facilitate the coal traffic, it is occasionally used to move empty stock, and for "specials". Class 40, "D200", is seen bringing a special slowly round the curve on 16 February 1985. (The bridges in the foreground previously carried lines into Stafford Road shed yard.)

(Brian Robbins)

36. A Gas Works Shunter.

Representing the small industrial locomotives which operated in various factories or works in and around Wolverhampton, is this picture of Wolverhampton Gas Company's 0-4-0ST named "Carbon", seen standing in the Gas Works complex, off the Stafford Road, in the 1950s. "Carbon" was built by Bagnall's, of Stafford, No.1673 of 1902, and survived until the early 1960s. The Gas Works possessed quite an extensive railway system, with sidings connected to both the GWR and LMS lines. Gas making ceased after Wolverhampton was converted to Natural Gas, and the buildings were demolished in the late 1960s and early 1970s.

(Industrial Railway Society)

37. Outside the High Level Station,

The High Level Station, built in the 1850s for the LNWR's Stour Valley line from Birmingham New Street to Bushbury, had a building designed by Edward Banks in the Italianate style favoured by the Shrewsbury & Birmingham Railway, with whom the LNWR had intended to share the station. This was swept away in the 1960s when the station was rebuilt and the railway was electrified. Note that the signs erected along the canopy advertise the services of the three pre-grouping railway companies that eventually served the town: the Great Western, the Midland, and the London & North Western Railways. This picture was taken about 1910 and horse-drawn vehicles occupy the station forecourt. It is possible that these vehicles were built locally at Forder's carriage works in Cleveland Road.

(Wolverhamton Public Libraries)

38 & 39. Butler's Brewery Transport

Butler's first motor lorry, a three ton dray, was a Hallford, photographed here at the Springfield Brewery in 1910. Left to right: E.Bagnall, W.Field, R.Hodson. The vehicle's life came to a sudden end when it crashed over the side of the Hermitage Hill, Bridgnorth, in January 1912. Hallford lorry chassis were built by J & E Hall Ltd. of Dartford, and were chain driven to the rear axle, the chain case is just visible. Many such vehicles were supplied to the War Department during the First World War.

Opposite: Mr.Monk, of Wolverhampton Motor Services handing over a Commer van to Mr.H.R.Luce of Butler's Brewery Garage Department, late in 1949. The gates of the Springfield Brewery are now listed. The brewery itself first opened on the site in 1873, but was greatly extended many times during the 1880s. The fine gateway into Cambridge Street, seen here, was not completed until 1899.

(Pictures from Butlers Magazine, via John Spittle's collection)

40 & 41. British Road Services in Wolverhampton.

BRS, the nationalised road transport undertaking was created in 1948, and had a depot in Wolverhampton in Steelhouse Lane. Logically, this was one of the Midlands Division, Birmingham District, Depots, originally coded 11E, although later re-coded ED. The local fleet included vehicles built by Leyland, AEC, Seddon, Foden, Guy and Atkinson. Two examples are shown: On this page - a Wolverhampton product, Guy "Invincible" articulated tractor unit 743 LOA, lacking its BRS fleet number and cabside crest, with a load of scrap metal for re-processing at one of the local steelworks, at the depot in 1963.

On the right - a classic lorry, a Foden rigid eight wheeler platform lorry, fleet number 1E6, smart in BRS red livery, parked in the depot yard in 1960. The cooling tower of Wolverhampton's power station, in Commercial Road, dominates the background of the picture.

(Both pictures: Simon Dewey)

42. Wright Brothers - "At Your Service".

During the Inter-War years the motor lorry's role in carrying freight long distances expanded enormously, and haulage contractors built up impressive fleets. The vehicles belonging to the Wright Brothers were turned out in a dark red livery, with black mudguards, and in this picture, three vehicles are lined up outside the Crown Street Depot. Claude Wright appears on the extreme right of the picture. From left to right the vehicles are: an Atkinson, a Foden of the late 1930s, and an earlier Foden.

(Claude Wright via John Spittle)

43. Locomotive in Transit

This Foden tractor unit was bought by Wright Brothers, of Crown Street, Wolverhampton as a four wheeler and rebuilt by them as a tractor to pull a Tasker trailer. This is a Wartime photograph, note the nearside headlight is masked, and the driver can be identified as Billy Kyle. Identifying the locomotive is more difficult! It appears to be Andrew Barclay 0-4-0T (1615 of 1918) that worked for Wm. Beardmore of Dalmuir. Arnott Young took over part of their Dalmuir works during the War and it appears that the locomotive became theirs. It could be in transit to IMI Witton about 1943, where the locomotive worked until the 1950s. The Foden looks smart in its dark red livery with yellow flash.

(Claude Wright's collection via John Spittle.)

44. Collected Just in Time.

Wright Brothers built up a large fleet of vehicles, and took delivery of three Maudslay trucks during the War, two eight wheelers and a four wheeler. Claude Wright collected this Maudslay Mikado, DDA 631, from the Coventry factory just a few hours before the factory was bombed! It can be seen in this Maudslay advertisement, used in the January 1941 Commercial Motor magazine, in its deep red livery with yellow flash. Note the masked offside headlight and the regulation absence of any bulb in the other headlight. One of the vehicle's first jobs was to rescue a broken down Albion lorry at Tern Hill, and fully loaded, and not "run in", it had to tow the eight wheeler back to Wolverhampton.

(John Spittle collection)

45. Delivering Potatoes.

Trucks delivering products to wholesale markets are often very well turned out. In Wolverhampton, Sammy Hyde's potato wagons, in red and gold livery, were often so attractive that he could sell the wagon as well as the potatoes he was carrying! Len Thomas worked for Wally White's Potatoes until able to set up on his own with two or three wagons. This Commer truck from the Rootes Group was in the same class as the firm's Humber Super Snipe, and looked very smart in Len's green and cream livery. Len himself apparently eventually emigrated to Australia.

(John Spittle collection)

46. Scammell Ready for Work

This Scammell Routeman has a "Designer-styled" cab, and has been freshly turned out by A.Comer Ltd., of Stonefield, Bilston, for Tarmac, the well known Wolverhampton based civil engineering firm. The vehicle is parked outside A.Comer's works for an official photograph. Albert Comer had begun his bodywork business by building caravans for fairground folk and developed the commercial vehicle body-building and coach-painting over the years.

(John Spittle Collection)

47. An Elegant Karrier.

This Karrier van was supplied to Contactor Switchgear for use as a demonstrator vehicle towards the end of the 1950s. It was usually driven by Jeff Griffiths, and was smartly fitted out inside with examples of the company's electrical products. Externally the beautiful coachwork was always kept spotless, and it looked very smart in its livery of two shades of grey with white lettering.

Contactor Switchgear Ltd. was founded in 1936, and established itself in Moorfield Road, Blakenhall. The company's machine shop, established in 1943, was in the building where the Sunbeam record car had been built. After numerous take-overs and recession-based problems the "Switchgear" closed in 1986.

(John Spittle's collection)

48. Bridge Repairs in Cannock Road.

The trolleybus routes to Bushbury Hill and Low Hill passed along the Cannock Road, where, close to the junction with Stafford Street, the road was crossed by two adjacent railway bridges. The first carried the GWR tracks into Herbert Street Goods Depot, the second carries the LMS High Level - Stafford main line. On an unidentified date in the late 1950s, three Wolverhampton Corporation tower wagons are seen providing access to work on the overhead wiring during repairs to one of the railway bridges. The Corporation owned several tower wagons built by Guy's. On the left is WDA 302, on the right are EUK 770 and WDA 301. (EUK 770 was one of a pair of vehicles supplied in 1947.) Standing on the railway bridge is ex-LMS Stanier "Black 5" 4-6-0, No.45310, of Bushbury shed.

(Phil Lycett)

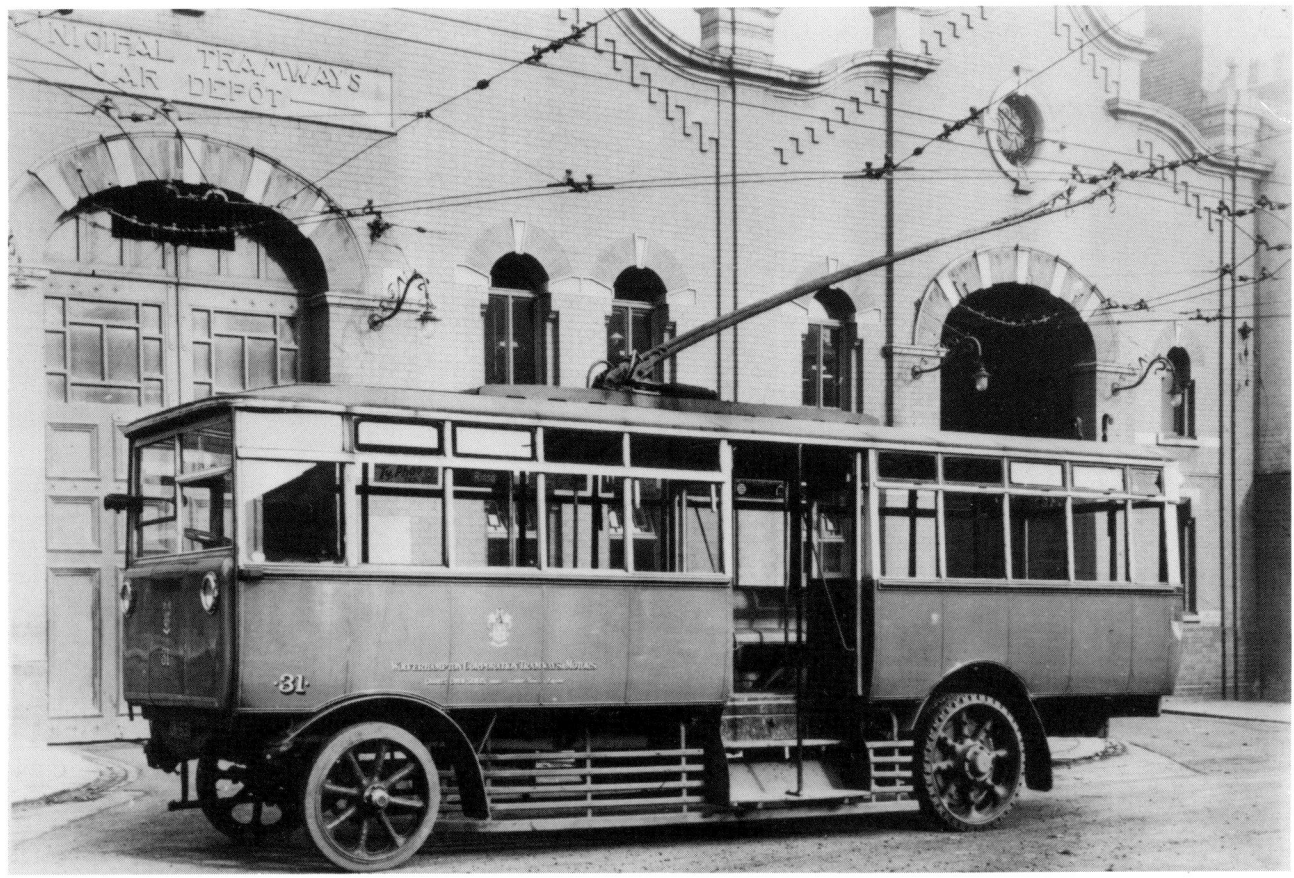

49. An Early Trolleybus.

Use of trolleybuses in the town began in 1923 when the tram route from Prince's Square to Rookery Bridge at Wednesfield was converted to trolleybus operation, and extended to Pinfold Bridge. Single decker, No.31, a Tillings Stevens vehicle with Dobson body seating 36 passengers, is seen outside the Cleveland Road Depot in 1927, shortly after entering service. The dignified architecture of the depot is worthy of note, its role being clearly indicated in stone for all passers-by to see. Over the years the doors were crudely widened to provide access for larger vehicles. No.31 remained in use until 1937, but well before then the solid tyred wheels were replaced with pneumatic tyres, an improvement no doubt much appreciated by passengers and crew alike.

(Millennium Collection)

50. Trolleybus Pride.

Wolverhampton Corporation was among the forefront of trolleybus operators in the country, and acquired a high reputation both nationally and internationally. At one time, the Wolverhampton system was the largest in the world. Here a group of trolleybuses and crews pose outside the Cleveland Road depot in about 1929, with No.58 prominent in the foreground. All the vehicles are Guy BTX six-wheel trolleybuses with Dobson bodies seating 61 passengers, delivered new between 1927 and 1929, and all withdrawn by 1940.

(Millennium Collection)

51. Trolleybus Demise.

Use of trolleybuses in Wolverhampton ceased on 5 March 1967, when the Dudley and Sedgley routes finally gave way to motor buses. Wholesale abandonment of the trolleybus system had commenced in 1963, although the route 32, (Oxbarn Avenue via Coalway Road), had already ceased on 21 May 1961. Between 1963 and 1967, the various trolley routes were taken over by motor buses, and withdrawn trolleybuses being towed away for scrapping became a regular sight. Here No.423, a Sunbeam, rebodied as recently as 1959, awaits being towed away in Hospital Street, just round the corner from the Cleveland Road Depot. The towing vehicle is an ex-Military AEC tractor unit, owned by the Corporation Transport Department.

(Phil Lycett)

52. Tettenhall Trolleybuses 1.

The conductor of trolleybus No.92 stands by his vehicle at the route's Tettenhall terminus, at the Upper Green, in the early 1930s. The bus is a Sunbeam six-wheeler delivered in 1932, and withdrawn in 1948, and the notice in the lower deck's third window from the rear appears to invite passengers to "make time for a trip to Beatties". The ornate waiting shelter, nicknamed the "Swiss Chalet", was built for the Wolverhampton Art and Industrial Exhibition, held in the West Park in 1902. It was transferred to Tettenhall for use as a tram shelter after the exhibition closed. The trolleybuses replaced the trams on route 1 in 1927, and in 1963 motor buses replaced the trolleys. The shelter survived until the early 1970s, when it was demolished as "unsafe".

(Millennium Collection)

53. Tettenhall Trolleybuses 2.

Trolleybus No.614 ready to leave for Tettenhall from the town centre terminus outside the old General Post Office, Lichfield Street, in the late 1950s. No.614 was typical of the last trolleybuses purchased by the Corporation during 1948 and 1949, all either Guy or Sunbeam vehicles with identical 8ft. wide Park Royal bodies. With most buses no wider than 7ft.6ins., the drivers' attention was drawn to their extra width by the fitting of white steering wheels. The old Post Office building is now in use by the Wolverhampton Polytechnic, but the elegant building between it and the Grand Theatre was demolished in the 1960s to be replaced by the present Post Office of rather undistinguished architectural style.

(Phil Lycett)

54. Prepared for War.

Wolverhampton Corporation Guy/BTX six wheel trolleybus No.74, photographed at Park Lane Depot during the Second World War. Note the masked headlights and white painted edges to the mudguards for running during the blackout. This Guy-bodied 59 seater vehicle was delivered new in 1931, and withdrawn in 1945. The predominantly green style of livery was introduced before the Second World War, but had disappeared by the 1950s. Vehicle No.78, from the same batch, was withdrawn in the same year and was sold to Don Everall for scrap. Somehow it escaped to Ireland, where it spent many years in the open in County Kilkenny, until dramatically "rediscovered". In 1990 it was towed back to the Black Country, not even pausing in Wolverhampton, but heading directly to the Black Country Museum, where its restoration will re-create one of these "piano-fronted" trolleybuses of the early 1930s, unique in the world of preserved vehicles.

(John Hughes collection)

55. Invasion from Bournemouth.

Bournemouth Corporation trolleybus No.168, a Wolverhampton-built Sunbeam with Park Royal body, of 1935 vintage, turns the corner from Lichfield Street into Stafford Street. This was one of twelve Bournemouth vehicles transferred to Wolverhampton to supplement the fleet during the War. The striking yellow livery was in contrast to Wolverhampton more muted shade of green. No.168 survived the War and returned to Bournemouth. The vehicles had come with their drivers, and at least one Bournemouth driver returned home with a bride from among Wolverhampton's conductresses. William Snape, the tailor on the ground floor of the Royal London Buildings supplied Norman Wisdom's famous suits - beautifully made, but ill-fitting!

(John Hughes Collection)

56. Huddersfield to Wolverhampton by trolleybus for 3d?

A bargain at more than twice the price! The red and cream Karrier six wheeler, Huddersfield Corporation No.541, already secured for preservation at the time, was visiting Wolverhampton specifically for use on a National Trolleybus Association tour of the remaining parts of the system one Sunday in May 1965. The vehicle is seen in Cleveland Road, having just reversed out of the depot, where it had spent the preceding night. Note how the depot's entrance has been widened since its early tramway days. Although Huddersfield commenced contraction of their trolleybus system earlier than Wolverhampton, they did not finally abandon trolleybuses until July 1968, over a year after Wolverhampton's last trolley had run.

(Simon Dewey)

57. First and Last.

Amy Davies joined Wolverhampton Corporation Transport in 1940 when conductresses were being recruited in the absence of male staff. In 1942 she was "directed" to become a trolleybus driver, and after three days training Amy was the first woman driver to pass the driving test, and thus became the town's first woman trolleybus driver. The photograph on the left was published in the Express & Star, to encourage other women to volunteer for such work during the War. On 5 March 1967, Amy had the distinction of also being the town's last woman trolleybus driver, seen here at the Dudley, Stone Street, terminus of route 58, with trolleybus No.437, a Roe-bodied Sunbeam of the late 1940s. On that day Wolverhampton's operation of trolleybuses ceased, Amy was transferred to other duties and retired in 1973. ("Expert opinion" in 1967 declared that women were not suited to the task of driving motor buses!)

(Express & Star and author's collection.)

58. Queen Square.

Trolleybus No.451 rounds the island that segregated incoming and outgoing traffic in Queen Square in the 1950s and 1960s, heading out on route 13 to Merry Hill, in the summer of 1963. Although the modern appearance of the Roe bodywork belies the Sunbeam vehicle's true age, it had entered service in 1947, originally with a Park Royal body. When it was rebodied in 1961 the passenger capacity was increased from 54 to 60. A total of 38 vehicles were similarly treated between 1958 and 1962. The Queens Cinema just edges into the picture on the right (see back cover), but was in use as a ballroom when this picture was taken. The road through Queen Square was rationalised in the late 1960s, and plans are currently under consideration for its almost complete pedestrianisation, although these have had to take account of a possible Metro route!

(Simon Dewey)

59. Court Road, Whitmore Reans.

A scene in the Spring of 1962, with trolleybus No.477 about to depart for Darlaston, via Bilston, on route 2. The full length trolleybus through route between Darlaston and Whitmore Reans, via Wolverhamton town centre, was instituted in 1930, replacing shorter routes. the route was converted to motor bus operation in 1965. Other items that have vanished from this scene are the Co-op Bakery electric delivery van, turning in the road, and two chimneys of Courtauld's Dunstall Factory, the site of which is now the Farndale Housing Estate.

A window cleaner's wheeled cart, sits "parked" on its nose to complete the picture.

(Simon Dewey)

60. Rainy Day at Fighting Cocks.
A bevy of trolleybuses at Fighting Cocks in 1961, with Roe-bodied No.431 to the fore, heading into Wolverhampton on the route 58 from Dudley. No.495, a Guy with an 8ft. wide Park Royal body is taking a party of trolleybus enthusiasts on a tour of the system. The Dudley, Sedgley and Fighting Cocks routes (58, 61, and 8, respectively) were the last trolleybus route in the town, ceasing on 5 March 1967, when No.446, a sister vehicle to 431, returning from Dudley just before midnight, had the distinction of being the last trolleybus to run on public service in Wolverhampton.

(Phil Lycett)

61. Off the Wires.

Mainly at the junctions in the overhead wiring, trolleybuses were occasionally known to become "dewired", their poles springing into the air, and bringing the vehicle to a halt. Long hook-ended bamboo poles were carried under the buses for use in retrieving dignity, and electric current, in such situations. One of the crew would have to fish in the air to catch the disconnected trolley arm, by hooking the metal ring at the end of the arm, pulling it down, and re-setting the skid contact under the wire. Ariel fishing is in progress here at the junction of Penn Road and Lea Road, where No.600, on the Penn Fields route has "dewired" in 1963. The photographer has his back to the Midland Counties Dairy, now replaced with a MacDonalds, but the Penn Road itself is unrecognisable to folks now familiar with the dual carriageway at this location.

(Simon Dewey)

62. Leicester Square, Whitmore Reans.

Virtually nothing of what can be seen in this picture now exists, other than the roadway, the northern side of Newhampton Road West back to Hunter Street having been redeveloped. A most notable absentee from the modern scene is the circular cast iron Gents' urinal visible on the right! Leicester Square was once the thriving centre of Wolverhampton western suburb, and even boasted its own cinema. Sunbeam trolleybus No.443 passes by in April 1965, heading into Wolverhampton on Route 7 to Darlaston.

The route was converted to bus operation on 9th August 1965.

(Simon Dewey)

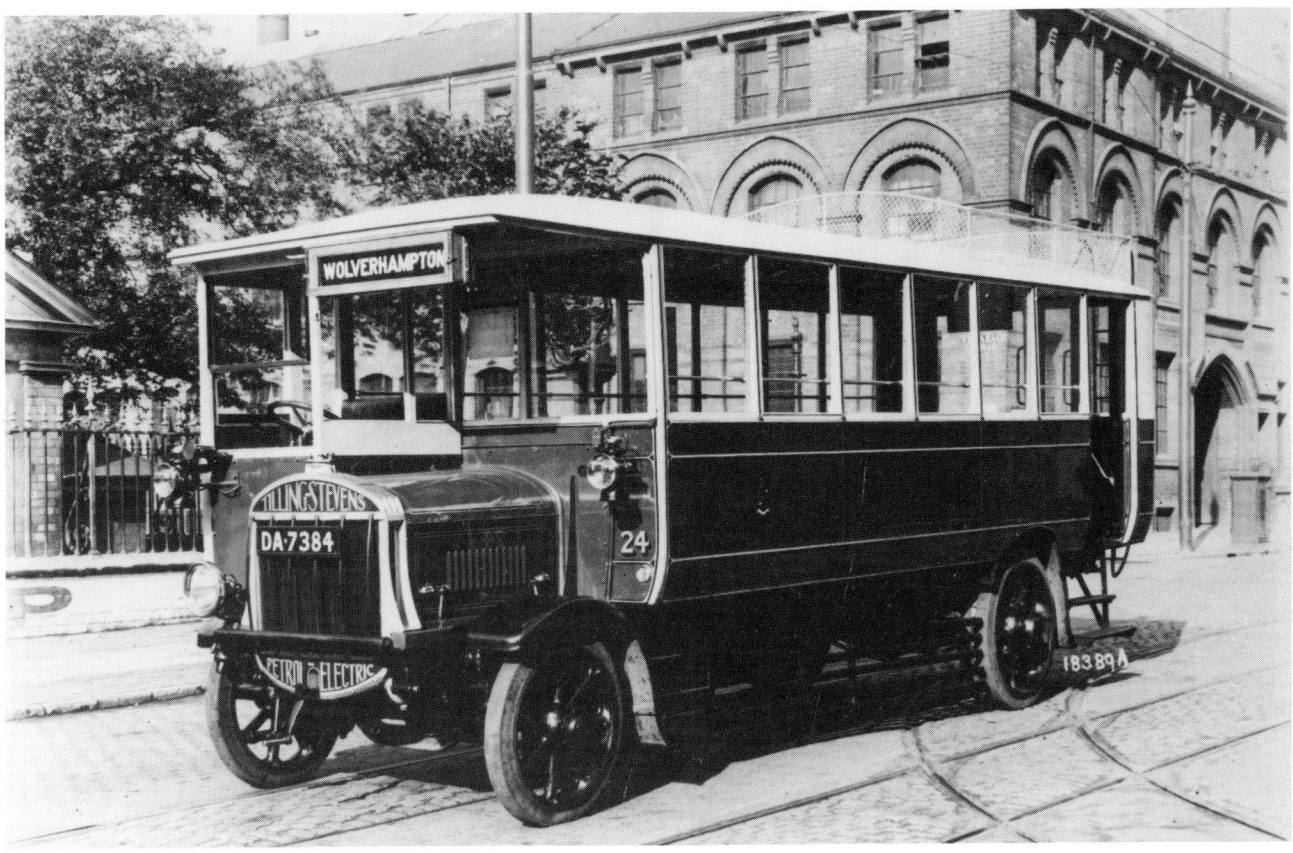

63. Tillings-Stevens Petrol-electric bus.

Tillings-Stevens single decker, with Thomas Tillings body, No.24, photographed in Cleveland Road between the depot and the Royal Hospital, in 1923. The newly delivered vehicle was the first to wear the apple green and primrose yellow livery in which Wolverhampton buses and trolleybuses are probably best remembered. The road is cobbled, and the ride in a solid-tyred bus must have been somewhat less than smooth!

Many of the Corporation's motor buses of the time were provided with roof luggage racks, a feature perpetuated on two Guy single deckers, No.s 566 and 567, as late as 1949.

(Millennium Collection)

64. Another "First" for Wolverhampton.

Wolverhampton Corporation's motor bus, No.47, of 1926, was the first six-wheel top-covered double deck bus in the country. It was built by Guy Motors with a Dobson body and had striking similarities with the first six wheeled top covered double deck trolley buses - including an open rear staircase. No.48, a "sister" vehicle also delivered in 1926 had an enclosed staircase, and from then onwards enclosed staircases became the norm. (on open staircases there was always the fear that the conductor or passengers could be thrown from the vehicle!)

No.48 is posed outside the old Town Hall, of 1871 vintage, and the bus, looking very new, may be taking the party down to the town's "Floral Fete", held annually in July.

(Wolverhampton Public Libraries)

65. Midland Red 1.

Midland Red's original garage in Wolverhampton was in Bilston Street. It was of rather limited size, and in the late 1950s and 60s a vacant site roughly opposite the Clifton Cinema (ie adjacent to the ABC, now Cannon/MGM) was used as an additional parking area. No.2091, a "SON" type single decker bus, built in the early 1930s, by the Midland Red Company itself, is seen parked opposite the Clifton in the late 1950s, withdrawn and awaiting scrapping. Midland Red (formally the Birmingham & Midland Motor Omnibus Co.) operated services from Wolverhampton to Stourbridge, Kidderminster, Stafford, Wellington, Ironbridge, Shrewsbury. Coseley, Oldbury, Dudley, and Birmingham.

(Phil Lycett)

66. Midland Red 2.

While Midland Red were famed for building their own distinctive vehicles prior to the mid 1960s, they also ran buses made by other manufacturers. Included in the fleet of the 1950s and 1960s was a batch of twenty Guy Arab double deckers built in 1949, and almost wholly of Wolverhampton origin, with Guy bodies and Meadows engines. These were No.s 3557 to 3576, and most spent their lives in and around Dudley. The final vehicle of the batch, 3576, is seen here awaiting to depart to Dudley, via the Broadway, in April 1962. It is standing in what was then the western end of Cleveland Road, and the Public Library can be seen in the background.

(Simon Dewey)

67. West Bromwich bus at St. George's.

Route 90, Wolverhamton to West Bromwich, was operated jointly by the Corporations of both County Boroughs, creating the only regular visits of West Bromwich buses into central Wolverhampton. While Wolverhampton's bus fleet was dominated by Guy vehicles, West Bromwich concentrated mainly on Daimlers. The livery of the latter fleet was also strikingly different, using two shades of blue, and cream, plus black and gold coach lining. No.228, a Daimler CVG 6, with Metro-Cammell body, awaits a return trip to West Bromwich at its terminus adjacent to St. George's Church. The church has survived as part of Sainsbury's supermarket, but the churchyard with its trees and hedges has disappeared under paving.

(Simon Dewey)

68. Country Routes 1.

Wolverhampton buses operated quite considerable distances into the countryside surrounding the town, with routes extending north and west as far as Bridgnorth, Wheaton Aston, and Weston-under-Lizard. The route to Bridgnorth, 17, originated as a GWR service from the Low Level Station in Wolverhampton to Bridgnorth Station, at both of which termini small bus garages were provided. The Corporation took over in 1923, initially using single deck buses, but introducing double deckers in 1939, when the terminal points were changed in each town. Although photographed in the War years, no.361 is seen posing with GWR staff and Corporation crews at Bridgnorth Station. Guy Arab 361 has a spartan "Utility" body, lacking any rear window to the upper deck, and the headlights are masked.

(Millennium Collection)

69. Country Routes 2.

Route 27 ran to Beckbury, operation being taken over by the Corporation from Midland Red in 1928. No.551, a Park Royal bodied Guy Arab, of 1950 vintage, enters the village in late 1964. This bus was one of the last batch of exposed radiator Guys in the fleet, (No.s 539 - 560), after which subsequent vehicles were either "tin fronts" or "full fronts".

(Doug Nicholson)

70. Bus Building at Park Lane.

Buses under construction at Guy's works in Park Lane during the late 1940s. Guy's were more noted for the production of commercial and public service vehicle chassis than for their body building, which was mainly undertaken under licence from other body manufacturers. The intended recipients of the double deckers on the left are unknown, but the single deckers on the right could well be destined for Wolverhampton Corporation, as they match the appearance of No.s 561 to 565, delivered in 1949. Attractive vehicles with their slightly flared body skirts, they frequently operated services to Churchbridge, Cheslyn Hay, and Bridgnorth via Ackleton. No.561 survived in use as a snow plough until about 1967.

(Millennium Collection)

71. St. James' Square.

Wolverhampton routes to Bilston (45), Moseley Road (70), New Invention (42), Ashmore Park Estate (72), Willenhall (5), and Walsall (29), all terminated in St. James' Square, which was also used a parking area for buses from other services between trips. The Walsall route was operated jointly by Wolverhampton and Walsall Corporation trolleybuses, two of the latter's fleet being visible in the right background, both 1947 built Sunbeams purchased in 1959 from Maidstone & District.

Other buses visible are Wolverhampton No.s 574 (a "tin-fronted" Guy double decker with a Roe body dating from 1953), 513 (a Daimler with a Brush body from 1948), and 565, one of five Guy-bodied Guy Arab III single deckers built in 1949. The leather radiator muffs on 513 and 565 are a noteworthy feature, regularly worn by many of the exposed radiator buses each winter.

72. Fallen on Hard Times.

Wolverhampton Corporation No.561, FJW 561, the last survivor of the batch of five Guy single-deckers with the Guy 34 seat bodies, No.s 561 to 565, delivered in 1949, was retained after withdrawal from revenue-earning service for use as a snow plough. A worthy and attractive candidate for preservation, it languished in a corner of the bus parking area in Oxford Street until about 1966 when it was sadly towed away to be scrapped. The photograph was taken in April 1965.

(Simon Dewey)

73. Open Platforms.

Front and rear views of Park Royal bodied Wolverhampton Guy Arabs, No.s 557 and 540 respectively, parked at Oxford Street in July 1970. These buses, delivered in 1950, were among Wolverhampton's last exposed radiator double deckers, although open rear platforms continued to be a feature of the next four types of "tin-fronted" vehicles purchased by the Corporation. In 1969 Wolverhampton Corporation's Transport undertaking was taken over by the West Midlands Passenger Transport Executive, and the Corporation's coat of arms was erased from the vehicles, to be replaced by the stylised "West Midlands" logo, visible in this picture. On the left is one of several ex-Birmingham City Transport Daimlers, brought in by the new operators to replace older Wolverhampton buses. WMPTE's blue and cream Birmingham-style livery was destined to be applied to many ex Wolverhampton buses, but only to two of the rear-entrance "tin fronted" vehicles, No.s 6 and 572.

(Simon Dewey)

74 & 75. Don Everall's Tours Ltd.

Don and Cliff Everall started their business in 1923, firstly providing a taxi service but, in July 1926, their first charabanc was acquired. The title, "Don Everall's Tours Ltd." came into use in 1934. By the outbreak of War they were operating thirteen vehicles. In this photograph, Don Everall himself is at the wheel of their first "chara", a 1926 Reo, (UK 1949), posed at the entrance to West Park. The vehicle was withdrawn in 1930. On the opposite page: This bold poster claims to illustrate "part of our fleet of luxury coaches", but the same two vehicles are printed three times in a clever piece of montage! Personnel and numberplates had been included in the montage to create "authenticity". It would appear that the vehicle on the right is an AEC Regal with Smith bodywork, purchased in 1932 (JW 1652), and its neighbour is another Regal of 1931 manufacture, with a Rushton & Wilson body (JW 64). Don Everall's ceased to be associated with coach travel in 1974 when the fleet was sold to National Travel.

(Don Everall Ltd.)

76 & 77. Football Coach.

Don Everall Ltd, Wolverhampton's major independent coach operator, supplied transport to the town's football team - the Wolves. In 1961 the company bought two new AEC "Reliance", Plaxton bodied, vehicles. One was for the Wolves team, and the other was for West Bromwich Albion, and these were used until 1965. 8282 JW, the Wolves' coach is seen here at the Company's yard when new. On the opposite page: Wolves celebrate winning the F.A. Cup in 1960 by touring Wolverhampton in Don Everall's AEC Regal IV with Yeates bodywork, of 1952 vintage (AEY 456).. It was new to Don Everall's West Bromwich subsidiary and came to Wolverhampton to be the Wolves' coach in 1958. It was withdrawn in 1961, when it was replaced by the above vehicle, and after being used by various other owners it was scrapped in 1966.

(Phil Lycett)

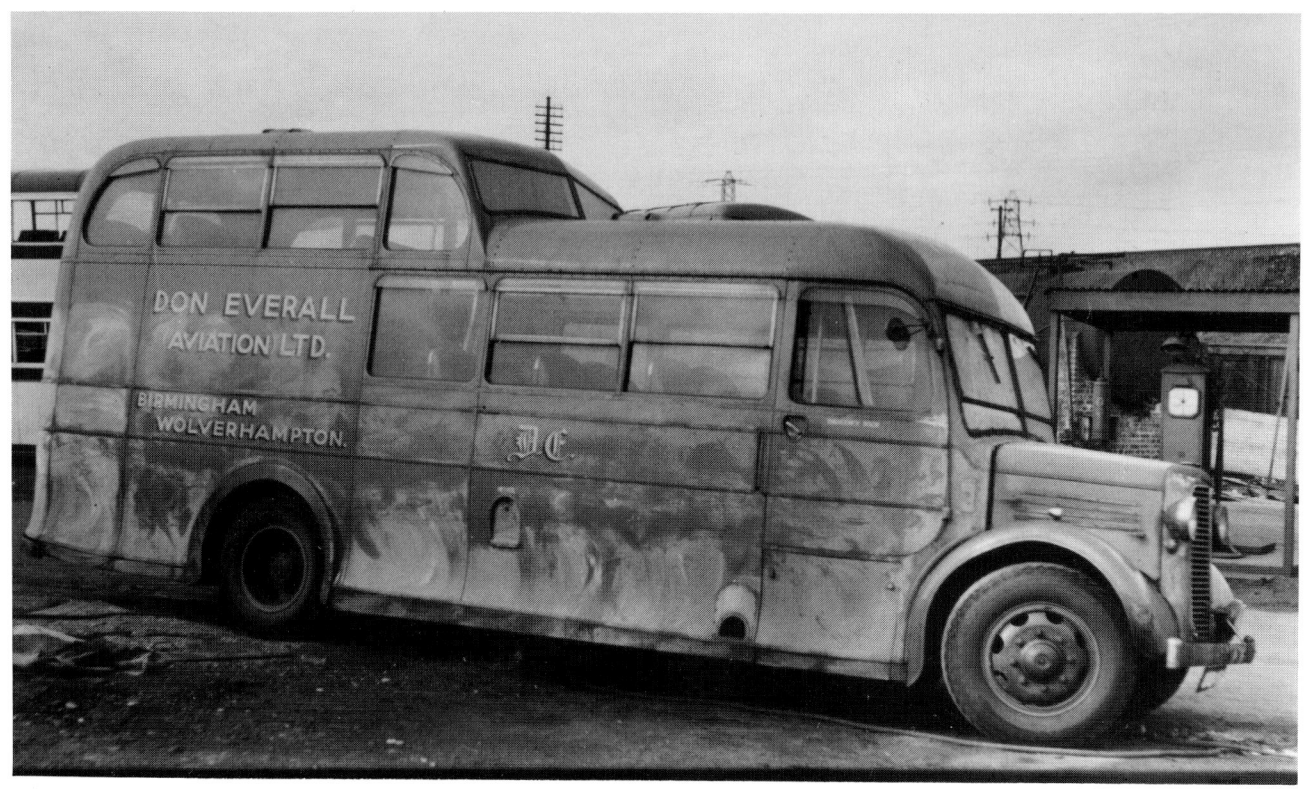

78. All Aboard for the Airport!

Wolverhampton Airport, at Pendeford, was opened in 1938. Normal services were suspended soon after, when it was used as a Wartime training ground for the RAF. After the War it returned to "municipal" ownership, and in 1950 it was the venue for the Kings Cup Air Race. It was managed, for the Corporation, by Don Everall (Aviation) Ltd., who also looked after the Wolverhampton Aero Club. Today the site is a housing estate and a business park! As if to create a "Heathrow" ethos to Wolverhampton's airport, Don Everall purchased two half-deck airport buses, the half deck at the rear creating a vast luggage hold. These Commer Commando vehicles with Park Royal bodies were supplied new to BOAC in 1946, and passed to BEA in 1947. They arrived in Wolverhampton in 1953, where they were used for the next five years. After their withdrawal in 1958, one of the vehicles is reputed to have become a mobile shop.

(Phil Lycett)

79. Cleaning the Street Lights at Snow Hill.

Midlands Electricity used this rather smart hydraulic lifting platform to reach the street lights when maintenance was required. The front half of the cut down Leyland half-cab single decker, ERA 918, provided accommodation for the crew. Photographed at Snow Hill, the background features the Central Library, opened in 1902, and on the right, the Gaumont Cinema, opened thirty years later. The Gaumont showed its last film on 10 November 1973, to be replaced by Allied Carpet's premises about seven years later.

The new building has changed hands again, and even Cleveland Road, obscured the vehicle, has become an extension of St.George's Parade.

(Phil Lycett)

80 & 81. Motoring in Style.

Vehicle Registration began in 1904, and the first number plate issued in Wolverhampton was DA 1. It was issued to a local solicitor, Mr.S.R.Rhodes, who is seen here at the wheel of his 1903 Ariel Tonneau. The passengers are his wife, sister, and son, ready to brave the elements in the early days of motoring. The number plate is now owned by his grandson and is still to be seen in Wolverhampton. (Dick Rhodes' collection)

Opposite: Wulfrunians not only rode about in cars - they built them. Many firms added car manufacture to their existing activities. For example, the Star Cycle Company introduced the "Starling" in 1905. In 1909, at the Star's Stewart St. Works, the Briton company was formed, under the direction of Edward Lisle Jnr., to produce a low-priced but sturdy range of cars. Ted Lisle is in the second car from the left in this line up of Britons, about 1910, possibly arranged as a Christmas card picture to advertise the Briton.

(Bert Bradford's collection)

82. Customised Bodywork.
By the First World War, the Star, of Wolverhampton, was one of the six largest motor manufacturers in the country. After the War private car production was resumed, and towards the end of the 1920s the company moved to a new purpose built factory in Bushbury. Ultimately the company came under the wing of Guy Motors. The purchaser of a Star had a choice of coachwork, and the Star Mercury illustrated here has quite unusual bodywork. The photograph was taken at the back of the Showell Road factory, at the end of the 1920s.

(Wolverhampton Public Libraries, via Alex Chatwin.)

83. The "Silver Bullet"

Sunbeam is one of the most famous names associated with Wolverhampton's vehicle industry, associated with the production of bicycles, motor cycles, cars, commercial vehicles, aero-engines, machine tools for the motor trade etc...the company originally being concerned with the Japanning and tin-plate trade when founded by John Marston. Many Sunbeam vehicular products were raced, and set out to break records. In 1927 the 200mph barrier was broken, and there followed a period in which the world land speed record changed hands several times in quick succession. By the beginning of 1930 the company had built the "Silver Bullet", over thirty feet long, but only three feet wide as a bidder for the land speed record. It is seen here, at the company's Blakenhall works, just prior to its departure for Daytona Sands, where it failed to break the record. At the end of the 1920s Sunbeam also produced a chassis suitable for a single deck coach, an early example of which is seen behind the "Bullet".

(*Wolverhampton Public Libraries, via H.Onion.*)

84. Bob's Taxis.

Bob's Taxis had offices at 88 Molineux Street, and 55 Clifford Street, and ran a smart fleet of Austin private hire vehicles in the 1950s. GDA 113, seen at front of this line up was new to Bob Williams in June 1948. They are thought to be lined up on Newhampton Road.

(Wolverhampton Public Libraries)

85. Clyno Staff Outing.

The first Clyno motor cycles were not built in Wolverhampton, but they had engines supplied by the Stevens Brothers. As the latter vacated their Pelham Street works, Clyno moved in. Before the First World War they talked of going into car production but, in fact, did not do so until 1922. This picture of the Clyno Staff Outing to Stourport in 1915 therefore only features Clyno motor cycles and sidecars. The large school building in the background, in Brickkiln Street, still stands today.

(Jim Boulton's collection)

1932 WOLF 1932

VIXEN 148 cc. DOUBLE-PORT LONGSTROKE. 15/- TAX.

SPECIFICATION.—*contd.*

Accessories.—Full kit of tools, inflator, and tin of oil.

Weight.—Complete with Standard Equipment, 192-lbs.

Lighting.—Villiers Direct Lighting, complete with 6-in. head lamp, and tail lamp, separate battery for parking lights.

Lifting Handle.—Fitted in a very convenient positon over the rear guard.

MODEL No W. 5. "VIXEN" Double-Port.   CASH PRICE **£25-10-0**

MODEL No. W. 6. as above but with Chromium Plated Tank Panelled Blue—Front and Rear Guards enamelled Blue to match. Rims Chromium and Centred Blue.   **£27-0-0**

87. Arthur Simcock and Sunbeam.

When sunbeam first produced motorcycles they had the reputation of being gentlemen's machines, with their oil-bath crankcases and elegant all black finish. However, their sporting models enjoyed great success, and in 1914, 1927 and 1928 Sunbeam won the Senior TT Team Prize. Seen here is Arthur Simcock, winner of the 1929 Austrian six-hour Grand Prix, on his Sunbeam motorcycle, which had maintained an average speed, for six hours, of over 60mph. Later Arthur Simcock was associated with Wolverhampton Speedway.

(Jim Boulton's collection)

88. The Penn Nib

Bill Boulton was proprietor of a small garage on the Penn Road. Later he moved to larger premises near the top of Lloyd Hill (now a Fina station), and there he built a few "Pen Nib" motor cycles, in both two and four stroke versions. He is seen here on one of his machines - note the solid forks and unguarded chain - about 1922. In 1925 he sold the garage and went to work for AJS as a road tester. His son, Jim Boulton, has worked hard to put Wolverhampton's vehicle industry "on the map" in his "Powered Vehicles of the Black Country" and "Wolverhampton's Cycles & Cycling".

(Jim Boulton's collection)

89. Line up at AJS.

The Stevens Brothers were successful manufacturers of motor cycle engines at their Pelham Street works. After a move to Retreat Street, the first AJS motor cycles were announced, and appeared in 1910. Forming a new company in 1914, production moved to Graisley, and Graisley House, seen in the background of this picture became the administrative offices of the company. The picture was taken about 1926, and on the left is one of AJS's experimental cars, with, on the extreme left, Tommy Jones, the AJS production manager, leaning against it. On the right of the car is Joe Stevens. On the third motor cycle from the left is G.H.Bradford, as seen in the Star cycle picture.

(Bert Bradford's collection)

90. The Star Cycle Company.

Edward Lisle was a pioneer in the world of cycle manufacturing, and produced cycles under the trade name, "Star". Production began in 1896 in Stewart Street, and by 1904, Star was Wolverhampton's largest cycle works. This picture illustrates the company's stand at a trade fair, about 1905. On the left is G.H.Bradford, who joined the company as a salesman, and ultimately became Sales Manager. The Sales Manager at the time when this picture was taken was Vic Calcutt, third from the left, who was run over by a tram at Penn Fields.

(Bert Bradford's collection)

91. Ride Criterion Cycles.

George Dugmore established his shop in Bilston Street in 1904 while in full-time employment with Bayliss Jones & Bayliss. The shop illustrated was his third premises, and it was here that he built up his own "Criterion" cycles. He died in 1919, at the age of 39, and his wife had to take over the business, assisted by Ethel, the eldest of four daughters. The photograph was taken in 1912. Left to right: Dorothy Dugmore, second oldest daughter, who later ran the business for a time, Mrs. Susan Dugmore, George Dugmore, daughter Ethel with her miniature Rudge Whitworth cycle, and cycling hat, and Harry Evans, the errand boy about to take a wheel to a plater. Mr. and Mrs. Dugmore's Elswick bicycles are parked at the kerb. About 1910, George Dugmore had been offered the Ford dealership, but he turned it down as he thought a better future lay in selling cycles. Another local cycle retailer, Ben Billingham decided to give selling Ford cars a try.

(Dorothy Hughes/Ethel Wild's collection)

92. Here Comes the Fair!

Three times a year the Brickkiln Patch, now the site of the Retail Market was used to hold fairs in Wolverhampton. (The fair moved to this site from St.Peter's Square just before the War.) The fair was presented by Pat Collins, the well known showman established in Bloxwich. In the 1950s, when this picture was taken, the fair was often transported and accompanied by a great variety of interesting second hand vehicles such as the ex Birmingham City Transport Daimler bus (AOP 707), of 1935 vintage, seen on the left with its roof lowered to the waistline of the top deck. On the right is one of the two Scammell "Showtrac" vehicles, supplied new to the Pat Collins firm just after the War. LDH 253 was named "The Major", after the showman's engine that it replaced, and was driven by Jack Harvey, manager of the Dodgems that make up the load. The full story of Pat Collins' life and the history of his fairs is about to be told in a forthcoming Uralia Press publication.

(Phil Lycett)